WEIGHT TRAINING
for
Runners

WEIGHT TRAINING
for
Runners

Ardy Friedberg

A FIRESIDE BOOK
Published by Simon and Schuster
New York

The author gratefully acknowledges permission to quote material from the following works:

—Lenore R. Zohman, M. D., *Beyond Diet . . . Exercise Your Way To Fitness and Heart Health*, American Heart Association, 1974, p. 6.

—*Physical Fitness Research Digest*, President's Council on Physical Fitness and Sports, Washington, D. C., Series 3, N. 1, January 1973.

—*Physical Fitness Research Digest*, President's Council on Physical Fitness and Sports, Washington, D. C., Series 4, No. 1, January 1974.

—Dr. Per-Olof Astrand, *Textbook of Work Physiology*, McGraw Hill, New York, 1977, p. 404.

—Dr. James A. Peterson, "Total Conditioning: A Case Study," *Athletic Journal*, Vol. 56, September 1975.

A Fireside Book
Published by Simon and Schuster
A Division of Gulf & Western Corporation
Simon & Schuster Building
Rockefeller Center
1230 Avenue of the Americas
New York, New York 10020
SIMON AND SCHUSTER and colophon are trademarks of Simon & Schuster
Designed by H. Roberts Design
Manufactured in the United States of America
Printed and bound by Halliday Lithograph
1   2   3   4   5   6   7   8   9   10
Library of Congress Cataloging in Publication Data
Friedberg, Ardy.
   Weight training for runners.
   (A Fireside book)
   1. Weight lifting.   2. Running—Training.   I. Title.
GV546.F74   796.4'1   81-14399
   ISBN 0-671-43174-9   AACR2
Photographs by Paul Schneck

Acknowledgments

Special thanks to Bill Curry at Diversified Products in Opelika, Alabama, who supplied all the equipment used in the photographs. And thanks to Karen Huston of Brooks Shoe Company who supplied the running clothes and shoes.

Also thanks to the models, Carol and Greg Frost, avid runners who became avid weight trainers; to photographer Paul Schneck for his eye, his patience, and his sense of humor; and to Susan Groberg whose manuscript typing was flawless.

Finally, thanks to Angela Miller—runner, supporter, and editor—whose interest made this project possible.

To Susie, with love and thanks for the constructive criticism and the constant encouragement.

Contents

Introduction

Physical fitness and running are not synonymous. Many runners think they are. They put on their running shoes and dash out the door in a hurry—determined to get in the almighty required mileage. Running contributes greatly to a fit cardiovascular system, to weight control and general body toning, but it isn't enough by itself.

The exercise enthusiast, whether a fun runner or a world-class marathoner, needs to balance his/her exercise program—to pay attention to not just the cardiovascular system, but also the musculo-skeletal system. Running strengthens the anti-gravity muscles (hamstrings, calves) but does little for the muscles in the front of the body (abdominals, quadriceps). This imbalance contributes to many injuries. A thorough fitness program would involve stretching exercises to prevent the shortening of the anti-gravity muscles and strengthening exercises for the opposing muscle groups.

Proper weight training can help prevent injuries and strengthen the body for better health and better performance. The strength of the quadriceps, for example, will help the novice runner pick up his/her knees so that he/she can more easily negotiate that hill in the park. The competitive runner will also find, for example, that increased strength in the quadriceps will result in better knee lift in the late stages of a long-distance race.

Increased upper-body strength is also helpful to a runner. Arm drive helps propel the runner forward. In the late stages of a marathon, when attacking hills, or in the finishing kick in a race, a more pronounced arm drive that has been made more effective through weight training can make a significant difference in a runner's performance.

Weight Training for Runners is an excellent guide for two levels of runners. For those who run for enjoyment and wish to follow an all-around fitness program, the book is a guide to achieving a balance of fitness that involves overall musculo-skeletal and cardiovascular conditioning. For those who wish to improve their race times, the book will provide an edge over the competition who might be a little weaker in the arms or legs at critical points in the race.

The book is especially valuable to women runners. Women usually have a less developed muscle makeup than men, and they often grow up not using the upper body in sports. Thus they can be remarkably underdeveloped above the waist, no matter how many miles they run. Dramatic improvement in running performance is often possible for women who develop at least a minimal amount of upper-body strength. The women of the elite racing team that I coach—Atalanta New York—have benefited greatly from weight training.

Two of the runners whom I coach have needs that are fairly typical of the average runner. One woman, who was out of action due to a series of running injuries, found after following a strict weight-training program that she not only minimized the risk of further injury, but also could run faster. A man I often train with was only running 50 miles a week, but he was getting much stronger than I was in our workouts. Finally he admitted it—he had been biking regularly and practicing weight training three times a week. The combined overall fitness program improved his particular fitness level more than if he had just upped his mileage to 70 miles per week.

Now it is time for me to practice what I preach. When I was running my best times I was doing weight training. Now I can utilize the tips in *Weight Training for Runners* to help me return to my former fitness levels.

Robert H. Glover
Author of *The Runner's Handbook*

WEIGHT TRAINING
for
Runners

1
A Personal Discovery

I started to run in 1977. Like most people I began in a very modest way, testing to see: (a) if I could do it; (b) if I liked it; and (c) what running could do for me. In those days it was a few miles a week at about a 9-minute pace—sometimes slower. If I covered 10 miles in any 7-day period, I thought I was really putting out.

I soon learned that the answers to questions (a) and (b) were "yes" and the answer to (c) was "take off weight," "give me some solitude," and "give me blisters on the balls of my feet."

My mileage began to mount steadily to 20 miles a week and then to 30, and aching knees joined the blisters. One thing led to another, miles piled up, and before you could say "George Sheehan," I'd signed up for the 1979 New York City Marathon.

I trained by putting in my miles, eventually working up to 90 a week at an 8-minute pace, and running a few short races and a half marathon. It wasn't a lot of fun putting in all those miles and spending all that time—at least an hour and a half a day—dodging cars and potholes, getting soaked in the rain and burned by the sun. But the blisters were finally replaced by calluses and the knees seemed to adjust to the pounding (replaced by aching shoulders and neck); and besides, I had read enough to know that running the marathon was going to be an exhilarating experience filled with camaraderie, a sense of purpose, and topped by a feeling of personal accomplishment akin to winning the Nobel Prize.

As the race neared, I'd lost about ten pounds and my legs were like rods of steel. Mentally I was ready and physically I felt strong and self-assured.

I kept pretty much to my race schedule, finishing in 3:41; and after recovering the power of speech I expressed my pleasure with myself, thanked myself for persevering on those long training runs, and told myself I'd never run another marathon.

My reasoning was simple: The open road was boring, the aches were minor but bothersome, the mental effort it took to finish the last 7 miles hadn't been worth it, and there had to be a better way to stay in shape that didn't include learning all the side streets in Manhattan.

That winter I ran a little, but without enthusiasm. And then I began writing a weight-training book with Mike Mentzer, a former Mr. Universe. While researching and writing *The Mentzer Method to Fitness*, a weight-training program for men and women, I began to do some weight training on my own. At first I was just trying to get the feel of things, the better to explain them. Then I began to really enjoy the weights. My own weight stayed the same, I began to build some muscle, and I was feeling strong and generally healthier than when I was running 60 to 70 miles a week.

Winter turned to spring and it came time to apply for the 1980 marathon. Encouraged by a running friend, I decided to go ahead and apply despite the lingering memory of that interminable and painful trot down Fifth Avenue and the exhausted feeling at the finish. As I dropped the application in the mailbox (my friend went to the post office to be sure), I was secretly hoping that it would either get lost in the mail or that I'd forgotten to fill in some important blank and my card would be thrown out. I was accepted.

The long training program began once again. I started to put in the miles, but at the same time I was continuing to work out with the weights.

I quickly discovered that I wasn't able to run and lift weights every day. A 10-mile run followed by a 20-minute workout with the barbells left me too exhausted to eat or read or carry on a decent conversation. I did get a lot of sleep, though.

Of course, it's no wonder. The body does have limited energy resources and all mine were being used every day with no time for recovery. To compensate, I set up a regular routine that consisted of 4 days of running, workouts with the weights on 2 of the alternate days, and a 1 day off each week. If the weather was particularly miserable, I'd substitute a heavier weight session for a run; and on those days (and there are those days) when I just didn't feel like running, I'd pump iron. I was concentrating on my upper body at the time, and the results were beginning to show. When running I felt stronger, and there was none of that tiredness or cramping in my shoulders and upper arms.

Regardless of progress, about 8 weeks before the race, I got very tired of running, and I made a decision. I would cut my mileage way back to 25 or 30 miles a week (usually three runs of 8 to 10 miles), increase work with the weights, and on race day I would run only as long as I felt good. I decided that the 59th Street Bridge (16 miles) would be the decision point, since it's one of the telling stretches in the race. I was mentally prepared to stop without guilt.

The day of the race was very cold and quite windy but not uncomfortable after you got moving. At 8 miles, still in Brooklyn, I felt strong but I was thinking about an abbreviated run. At the bridge I still felt fine, and though I didn't know if I was going to finish, I felt too good to stop. I had too much left.

Unlike the year before, when I lost everything at 18 miles, I was still going strong at 21 miles. Then, as it must happen, the glycogen is suddenly gone, and you begin to rely on instinct. I slowed down considerably, drank some water, and headed toward Central Park. My brain kept sending signals telling me to stop, but the body doesn't always listen. So I kept moving, watching the street numbers decrease ever so slowly from 135th to 130th to 110th and the northern edge of the park. It wasn't fun, and memories of the previous year began to surface again.

But, at 23 miles, just at the entrance to Central Park, I got a very pleasant surprise. It was starting to come back. I suddenly picked up my pace again and finished the last 3 miles strongly.

My time was 3:45—slower than the year before. But instead of that nauseated, slightly faint feeling, and the soreness that I had experienced immediately after finishing the year before, I was feeling very good. I didn't even have to sit down, I wasn't sore, and I felt mentally as if I'd accomplished something. My slower time was really of little consequence compared to my total physical and mental condition.

It didn't come to me immediately, but that evening I could only account for my performance in one way—the weight training. Of course, there are many runners and physiologists who could have told me that weight training is a significant aid to the runner and that many long-distance runners, including Olympic champion Frank Shorter, train regularly with weights. But I didn't know it at the time.

It took awhile to confirm my empirical evidence—but the results of that research are the foundation for the exercises in this book.

2
Running and Strength

According to physiologists and coaches there are six major elements in good athletic performance:

1. Skill
2. Speed
3. Mobility
4. Endurance
5. Motivation
6. Strength

The last element, strength, has only recently been included in this list; yet many coaches now go so far as to say that strength is the key to winning performance in any sport from football, to golf, to distance running. It has even become a sports truism that given two athletes or two teams of roughly equal skill and desire, the stronger will almost surely win. Why? Because three of the elements of good performance—speed, mobility, and endurance—are all functions of strength. Therefore, strength plus skill plus desire equals a combination that is nearly unbeatable.

So weight training, the only real strength builder, has finally been recognized for its value as a complete physical conditioner. The fact is that lifting weights in a regular program of exercises increases the strength of all the body's major muscles, improves speed and endurance, increases flexibility and mobility, relieves stress, and develops a great-looking body in the process.

With all these proven, positive benefits it's amazing that weight training has only recently emerged from the dark recesses of the basement, the attic, the garage, and the YMCA. For decades coaches, professional and amateur athletes, and people just interested in getting fit shunned weight lifting because they believed it was only useful if you wanted to be Mr. America and, worse yet, that it was actually detrimental to performance in sports.

The facts have always belied the myths and superstitions surrounding weight training; nevertheless, physical educators who should have known better were afraid that work with weights would hinder rather than enhance performance.

Running, in particular, was supposed to be restricted by muscular development (the old muscle-bound canard), and the weights were said to strain joints and tendons and make them less flexible at the same time, and to weaken backs and flatten feet.

Now, at last, all has been forgiven and weight training has achieved a new level of popularity in this country. Television carries weight lifting and bodybuilding events on a regular basis, muscle magazines have grown in circulation, physique shows draw large crowds, sales of equipment have skyrocketed, and bodybuilders have become international celebrities. A recent fitness survey, sponsored by Perrier, uncovered nearly 4 million people who said that they work out with weights on a regular basis; and there is certainly an equal number who lift occasionally.

Why have the blinders been taken off? There are several reasons: First, the recent successes of European sports teams who have long used weight training for most of their athletes; second, the accomplishments of individuals and teams who use weight training as a regular part of their conditioning programs (the Pittsburgh Steelers in football, the Ohio State University swimming teams, and Frank Shorter in distance running are just a few examples). Their progress has convinced even the skeptical coaches and physical educators. Today, nearly all professional teams have instituted strength programs and employ weight specialists. Many colleges and high schools have followed suit.

Third, and most important of all, the new popularity of "pumping iron" owes much to the advances in sports medicine and exercise physiology that have resulted from the rise of the fitness movement in this country and the acceptance of running in particular.

The "discoveries" that have led to a clean bill of health for weight lifting as a conditioning activity are really not new, but the estimated 90 million people now interested in physical fitness have given the old and new research an immediacy and importance it didn't have before.

Working with weights is a very individualized method of physical exercise. Much of what a person can do is determined by relative strength, and the type of training program used depends on the type of activity a person is training for. It's true that increased strength is beneficial for all athletes, but improved performance can only be achieved through a weight-training program specific to a given sport. Different programs are needed for tennis players, golfers, swimmers, or cyclists.

The program in this book *is* specifically designed for runners.

Of course, some of the exercises described here are quite similar to those for other sports. There are, after all, only 15 to 20 movements and variations needed to work all the body's major muscles. Most serious weight lifters know them all, and they also know which exercises benefit which muscle group.

Most runners don't know about weight lifting, and it's difficult and time consuming to put together a well-balanced, comprehensive program without some knowledge of the subject.

That's why *Weight Training for Runners* is different from all other weight-training and running books. The resistance exercises in this program were selected to meet the needs of the runner—to build strength for running and to help prevent common running injuries:

The workouts are divided into four categories:

Part I — Pre- (Post-) Run Warmups with Weights—7 minutes
Part II — Lifting on a Running Day—10 minutes
Part III — A Workout for Off-Days—20 minutes
Part IV — Lifting Instead of Running—25 minutes

Each workout can be used separately or in combination with the others. All the exercises build muscle but not bulk. They should be performed at least two or preferably three times a week.

Here's what this unique weight-training program, followed faithfully, will do for you:
1. Improve overall strength quickly and painlessly
2. Improve performance
3. Help prevent sports injuries

4. Help rehabilitate after injuries
5. Improve cardiovascular fitness
   (if performed properly)
6. Increase flexibility
7. Make you look better
8. Relieve mental stress

It follows, then, that weight training is the next logical step for anyone who wants to be completely fit.

3
Running and Weight Training and the Body

There is a story told about the Reverend Bob Richards, one of the world's finest all-around athletes in the 1940s and early 1950s. It clearly illustrates the benefits of weight training in general and its value for maintaining a high level of fitness in the absence of any other type of training program.

Richards was hospitalized for a minor operation while in training for the 1948 Olympics in which he represented the U.S. in the decathlon. While convalescing in bed, Richards worked his legs with weights attached to iron boots and exercised his chest and arms by pressing a barbell while lying flat on his back. Later, he gave public credit to weight lifting for helping him resume hard training shortly after his release from the hospital.

Renaldo Nehemiah, the current world-record holder in the hurdles, regularly trains with weights and is capable of bench pressing more than 300 pounds. Nehemiah says, "It's not the power in the legs that counts. I have more power in my upper body and that's where you really need it. The legs go where the arms take them."

Frank Shorter, Olympic marathon winner, and Grete Waitz, two-time winner of the prestigious New York City Marathon, both work out regularly with weights.

An even more dramatic example is Gayle Olinek, currently one of the top women marathoners in the world with a fourth-place finish at Boston to her credit. Olinek began serious training only two years ago at the age of twenty-five. Her training is a mixture of long and short, fast and slower runs, and weight training—including days when weight lifting replaces running completely. She says, "I believe in weight training because running to the exclusion of everything else makes you weak." Olinek, who has also competed in women's bodybuilding championships, has worked with all kinds of weight-training equipment from Nautilus to barbells, and says her speed has improved and she has suffered fewer injuries as a result.

Olinek is right, of course. Running wears the body down. The long-distance runner's public image is one of almost painful thinness—a strong (though thin) pair of legs supporting an upper body so spare you can almost see the heart beat. This image isn't far off the mark. You can't run 120 miles a week and end up with much in the way of muscle. Muscle fiber is torn by heavy exercise. Metabolic wastes of all kinds increase. Glycogen stores are depleted from the constant exertion, and blood-sugar levels drop. Water is lost through sweat, resulting in an imbalance of electrolytes that are vital to the central nervous system. Joints, tendons, ligaments and even bones are weakened. This is not a pretty picture.

Despite the depletion, fatigue, and stress of heavy exercise, however, the body continues to function at a lower capacity; and when the run is over, it immediately begins to reconstruct itself. It's this continuous process of tearing down and building up that creates the conditioned body.

Weight training has the same effect on the body as running. In weight training the tearing-down process results from continually overloading the muscles, calling on the muscles to handle greater weights as strength develops. During the reconstruction process following a workout with weights, however, the body not only rebuilds its glycogen stores and eliminates metabolic wastes, it also builds skeletal muscles and strengthens joints, tendons, and ligaments. And if performed with very little rest between exercises, it also improves cardiovascular fitness.

Advances in exercise and work physiology usually go unnoticed by even professional runners and coaches, so there is no reason to believe that people who run for fun or fitness or both ever read or hear about changes in training ideas.

That's why it's taken weight training for runners so long to catch up with the pack in this country. And as with any new concept, there is still considerable resistance. Most of it comes from the gurus of the running world who firmly maintain there is just no substitute for running, and nothing but running can make you a better runner. Their criticism isn't aimed as much at weight training itself as at the time and energy that weight training takes from the long, slow distance work which is supposed to be the only way to build a base for running races.

Well, running isn't all there is out there—despite what the gurus may say. There are other ways to get fit and stay fit. There are other exercise regimens that increase cardiovascular fitness and make you feel good.

Weight training is one of them. It's great to live a long time, but it is even nicer to live a long time and have a well-developed body to live in.

4
Fitness and Strength

Runners don't just run to cover the miles. If there are 20 million runners in the country, there are probably at least 40 million reasons why they run. The reasons range from meeting new friends to sleeping better, from improving creativity to getting away from the family, from losing weight to getting and staying fit.

Undoubtedly the most important reason for most people is overall physical fitness. The fact that running is good aerobic exercise is now chiseled in stone and serves as the First Commandment of the runner's religion. And why not? If the heart isn't fit, there is no such thing as having a fit body. Some doctors say heart fitness *is* physical fitness. In fact, the Perrier survey indicated that 90 percent of the population is convinced that people who exercise regularly are less likely to have heart attacks. Of course this has yet to be proved, but it's still the way that the public perceives exercise. The American Heart Association says fitness is "a state of body efficiency enabling a person to exercise vigorously for a long time period without fatigue and to respond to sudden physical and emotional demands with an economy of heartbeats and only a modest rise in blood pressure."

The *Physical Fitness Research Digest* has a less heart-oriented definition of fitness. Their official interpretation says fitness is, "The ability to carry out daily tasks with vigor and alertness, without undue fatigue, and with ample energy to enjoy leisure-time pursuits and to meet unforeseen emergencies."

In addition to cardiovascular fitness there are several other factors that affect the ability of a person to achieve physical fitness. They are:

1. Physical size and body proportions—height, weight, body type
2. The ability to release aerobic and anaerobic energy
3. Strength of the body's muscles
4. Available energy and potential energy from food
5. Flexibility

With the exception of body type (endomorphic—pudgy with soft muscles; ectomorphic—long and lean with stringy muscles; mesomorphic—broad shoulders and heavy bones with well-defined muscles) and height, these critical fitness factors can be controlled by the individual. A person can change weight through diet; the metabolic processes involved in the release of energy can be developed; the right foods can provide energy; flexibility can be improved by stretching; and strength can be increased by weight training.

In fact, running by itself will improve most of these elements. But running doesn't develop real muscular endurance or strength and it doesn't increase flexibility. The reason running doesn't increase muscular strength is that only one major muscle group—the legs—is being exercised. And muscular strength and muscular endurance are the same things. People with greater strength have greater endurance. Build one and you build the other.

The President's Council on Physical Fitness and Sports says it this way: "Improvements in absolute muscular endurance, motor ability elements, and athletic abilities are associated with the individual's muscular strength. Thus, strength development may be considered not only a physical fitness need but fundamental to the total physical being."

It seems obvious that only weight training can finish the job that running starts, and that weight training can develop the "total physical being" that's so desirable. And if the original premise is true, that you are running to get and stay physically fit, you aren't making it if you stick to running alone.

Even the legs aren't getting the proper stress to develop muscular strength. To be totally effective, exercise movements have to continue through the entire range of the muscles' ability to move. This is why isometrics really don't work. They will make you stronger if you perform them correctly, but only in the contracted position in which you do them. So, if you push your hands together you'll get stronger and increase your ability to push things together with your hands, but the rest of the arm's musculature isn't benefiting.

You experience the same thing with running. When you do your stretching exercises after running (you *do* do them of course?) you have a little trouble reaching your toes, much the same as you had when you warmed up before running (you did, didn't you?). You're actually stiffer than you were when you started. This is because your muscles have been exercised but not in their full range of motion; and they have actually stiffened in other positions.

The exercises in this book will put your muscles through that full range of motion. They will help you develop strength and endurance, they will make you a better runner, they will make you more physically fit, they will make you look better, they might even change your mind about weight lifting as a total fitness sport.

You won't have any trouble touching your toes after you work out with the weights.

5
What to Expect

The problem with exercise programs, like diet programs, is that so many have come down the pike and promised so much that it's hard to decide whether to try another one or not. But, for the most part, the blame for the failure of programs of fitness or weight control does not usually lie in the regimen itself, but in the unrealistic approach of those who want to improve themselves.

Running instruction books, with few exceptions, are not written for the average runner. It's not unusual to find graphs, charts, schedules, and training routines that include sprints, long- and short-distance runs, interval training, and a combination of all of them. Bill Rodgers would be confused by the intricacy of most of it all, and the average runner who is not a mathematician takes one look at the imposing and time-consuming training sequences and gets discouraged. There are weekly goals, monthly goals, even yearly goals that lead to the 2:30 marathon we're all capable of. This kind of schedule is for professional runners. Trying to run someone else's pre-set times makes a person feel downright inadequate, and that type of unrealistic goal setting accomplishes little.

In weight training, however, it's quite easy to set realistic goals for a desired level of fitness—goals that are achievable. The weight trainer progresses at his or her own pace, not comparing the results to anyone. If you find you can lift a certain weight for a given exercise, that's the weight you can use—not one taken from a chart for your weight and height or some other arbitrary method. In developing strength the goal is just to get stronger and continue to get stronger.

The following chart (see p. 28) can be used to assess your progress and keep track of your body weight, the amount of weight you are using for each exercise, and the number of sets and repetitions you're performing. But as you can see, you fill in the chart.

Here are the realistic results you can expect from following the program in this book:

—An increase in overall strength/balanced musculature
—Increased upper-body strength
—Greater endurance
—Stronger legs
—Improved flexibility
—Reduction of body fat

Let's look at these expectations one at a time.

BALANCED MUSCULATURE

It's a fact that most runners have relatively weak upper bodies. Most women have limited upper-body strength to begin with, and women runners are no exception. A good test of strength is the pull-up. If you can do a pull-up or chin, just one, you are in better than average shape. So you can easily see that most people have a long way to go.

Runners do have a jump on most other people who take up weight training for the first time because the legs, at least the frontal thighs, are already fairly strong. The problem is the hamstrings, which are relatively weaker than the quadriceps in most runners. This imbalance can cause muscle pulls as the front of the leg overpowers the back.

The goal we're reaching for, however, is balanced development over the entire body; and the exercises that follow will provide that development in a short time.

You'll rather quickly increase the strength in your shoulders, arms, upper and lower back, hips, buttocks, and abdomen. All these areas are critical for the runner, and none of them gets any real exercise from running alone.

EXERCISE LOG

Exercise	Date	Sets	Reps	Weight	Remarks

Note: This chart can be duplicated and used for all the exercises in the book.

ENDURANCE

Muscular strength is determined by the amount of weight that can be lifted in a single maximum contraction of a muscle. Muscular endurance is related to the ability to continue to perform muscular contractions. This is why muscular strength improves muscular endurance. Distance running requires very little actual strength, possibly as little as 25 percent of the overall strength of the leg muscle. Research has shown that when the exerted force is below 15 percent of the muscle's maximum strength, the contractions can be continued more or less indefinitely. It's easy to see, then, that an increase of only 10 percent in muscle strength can add a heaping measure of endurance.

LEGS

The runner's leg strength is, of course, crucial to the ability to cover long distances; yet most runners have relatively undeveloped muscles, especially in the upper legs. This is mainly because the regulated stride, almost always performed at a steady rate, doesn't provide any muscle overload—the factor that increases strength. The leg exercises in this book increase resistance and force muscle growth. Strength improvement exercises are necessary for all muscle groups, despite the specificity of other exercise—in this case running. Mere repetitions of contractions that place minimal stress on the muscular system have little effect on the strength of the muscles involved.

FLEXIBILITY

Running does not improve flexibility. In fact, in extreme cases, it can cause muscle atrophy because many muscles, even in the legs, are unused or only moved through a shortened range of motion. Weight training, on the other hand, exercises all the body's muscles and, if performed correctly, extends and contracts the muscles as far as they will go without strain. This increases flexibility.

BODY FAT

Men have about 15 percent body fat distributed throughout their bodies and women have about 25 percent. The rest of the body is muscle, bone, tissue, and fluid. Running long distances reduces body fat, but weight training does too. One study reported by the President's Council on Physical Fitness and Sports reported that college women, on a regular program of weight-training exercises, improved body contours and showed a marked reduction in skin-fold and girth measurements.

Still, the principal results of weight training are higher levels of muscular strength and endurance. So you can see that you have much to gain and little to lose except that lean and hungry look.

6
Injury Prevention

T he runner's magazines, usually written for runners by runners, use half of each issue to tell people how to run and train, and the other half explaining how to treat the injuries that running creates—shin splints, tendinitis, joint and cartilage damage, knee problems, and bone bruises.

The force imposed on the ankle, knee, hip, lower back, joints, tendons, and ligaments with each stride can be as great as 2,000 pounds. It's no wonder there is so much talk and mystification about the "pain of running," sometimes called "the joyous pain of running," to give it a less depressing connotation.

Statistics have shown that running is among the most dangerous sports, with nine out of ten runners suffering some kind of injury in a 12-month period. Some of these injuries are caused by potholes, taxis, bicycles, and muggers, but most are the result of running itself. An activity that is so good for you shouldn't cause injuries.

You can prevent a certain number of running injuries by wearing good running shoes, warming up properly, and training sensibly—that is, not putting in excessive mileage. But the best way to prevent injury is to strengthen the entire body, including the lower body. You'll be surprised at how much better a runner you'll become.

Again, it's weight training to the rescue. Lifting weights itself is so safe when properly conducted that it is virtually injury free. But more importantly, the exercises in this book will develop the total body strength so necessary for stabilizing the pelvis, supporting the driving action of the legs and arms, reducing muscle fatigue that can result in stiffness in the shoulders, neck and upper back, and supporting the tendons and ligaments around the knees and ankles—the high-pressure areas where sprains, pulls, and tears are common.

Obviously, weight training offers no guarantee against injury. Nothing does. But it will make injuries less frequent; and when, and if, they occur, they will be less severe.

7
Some Basics You Should Know About

Weight training is a simple sport. Equipment is basic and inexpensive. It takes very little time, and the exercises can be done in a large closet if necessary. It's convenient, you don't have to wear any special outfits, it's private, it's satisfying, and it's rewarding. Not a bad little package.

There are some things you should know, however:

EQUIPMENT

You can get all the equipment you need for less than the cost of one good pair of running shoes. And buying a set of barbells and dumbbells is considerably less complicated than trying to sort through all the shoe ratings.

Weight-training equipment comes in sets—usually about 110 pounds of weight, including a bar, collars, sleeves, dumbbells, and plates. You can get a bigger set, but you probably won't ever need it. There is only one real decision you'll have to make, and that's whether to get the traditional iron plates or the newer vinyl-covered models. Vinyl is quiet and cheaper by about half. Metal is more compact and is virtually indestructible. Everything you need should cost less than $60, and is available at most sporting goods and department stores. (See Figure 1).

Figure 1: Barbell and dumbbell set

SEE A DOCTOR

You may be running regularly and think you're in good shape; but weight lifting puts a different kind of stress on the body, and it can be especially dangerous for someone with a heart condition. If you have any doubts, see your doctor before you touch a barbell.

OVERLOAD

Muscles grow when they are overloaded. Sprinters have well-developed thighs because the thighs get a lot of work in training. Weight training uses the same principle. At first, the weight you use for each exercise will be relatively light. After a few workouts, the beginning weight will feel so light that you'll think you can go on forever. That's the time to start making it a little harder for yourself by adding weight to the bar, and increasing the resistance that your muscles have to overcome. Muscles must be overloaded to grow.

ENDURANCE VERSUS BULK

If you want highly defined, bulky-looking muscles, you can do low repetitions with heavy weights. But as a runner you want to develop endurance as well as strength, and that means you'll be using lighter weights and doing more repetitions of each exercise. There is a good deal of research to show that the optimum number of repetitions for pure strength is 3 to 5 and for endurance it's 8 to 10.

DRESS

Wear loose-fitting clothes (your running clothes will do) so that there are no restrictions on your movements. It's best to wear shoes for stability and support. Your old running shoes will do just fine.

SORENESS

You're going to be a little sore after your first few workouts, but certainly no more so than you are after a particularly long or fast run. The muscles you'll be exercising in your upper body will be the sorest because they are exactly the muscles that are weakest in most runners. Don't worry about any stiffness or soreness, because it will go away in a day or two. If it persists, give yourself a couple of days off and start up again when there is no pain.

HOW LONG

The exercises in Part IV should take less than a half hour to complete. The other routines take 20 minutes or less. This time depends on how fast you move from exercise to exercise.

HOW HARD

Do the exercises as if you meant them—that is, don't go with weights that are too light (though it may give you a sense of accomplishment), and exert the same kind of effort that you would for a day's run.

OVERTRAINING

If you're running 100 miles a week and trying to work in some weight training as well, the chances are you're overtraining. In fact, the chances are you are running too much to start with. Overtraining is a real bugaboo because it's cumulative. If you continue to tax the body to its limits day in and day out, you're not getting more fit at all. You'll become more susceptible to injury, and your general resistance will be lowered until you find yourself on your back. It's the same with weights. Too much isn't better.

FORM

Good running form is essential to good performance, and the same is true with weight training. Sloppily performed exercises are not only unproductive, they can be dangerous because muscles are placed in unnatural positions, under considerable stress. Most exercises are performed with a straight back. Rounded shoulders are out. Jerking or bouncing the bar is also bad for the muscles involved; and if you use the momentum of the bar and the weights, you aren't getting the full benefit of the exercise anyway. It's helpful to check your form in a mirror from time to time to see if you're doing what you feel like you're doing.

WHEN

Right now you probably run at a specific time each day. Since that's the time you have set aside for exercise anyway, that's probably the best time to do your weight training. It doesn't matter if it's morning, noon, or night, just so that it fits into a regular schedule. You wouldn't run immediately after eating, so don't lift weights then either.

BREATHING

A lot of weight-training books make a great deal out of breathing in and out at the right time. It probably does work a little better if you breathe in as you push or pull the weight and exhale as you lower it to its starting position. In general, though, you'll breathe when you have to. The only thing you must not do is hold your breath. It doesn't help you move the weight and it puts a real strain on your heart.

WHERE

About 30 square feet of space is really all you need for these exercises. If you can find such a place that has light and air, you'll have a workout area that will meet all your needs. Of course, if you can set up a gym in your garage, basement, attic, spare room, bedroom, or other permanent area, that's even better because there is a certain psychological advantage to knowing what a space is for.

HOW OFTEN

How often to work out is pretty much up to the individual. You can use the warmup routine before every run, but it doesn't make sense to run for an hour and then work out for another half hour. If you want to use the more intense exercises in Parts II and III, allow at least 4 hours between the weight training and running. If you run in the morning, for example, then you can work out with weights at night, and vice versa.

AMOUNT OF WEIGHT

Begin with light weights—often the bar alone will be heavy enough—for all the routines in this book. There is no formula for determining how much you should use, so it will take some experimentation. Don't use such a light weight that you can do 20 repetitions or such a heavy weight that allows only 1 or 2. If you can do 8 to 10 reps with the last few being a little difficult, that is a good place to start. The idea is to work hard but not to strain.

PROGRESSIVE RESISTANCE

There is a classic story, probably apocryphal, that clearly illustrates the idea of progressive weight training. It concerns an ancient Greek herdsman who built his strength by carrying a newborn calf every day until it grew into a full-grown cow. He continued to overload his muscles with the increased weight and constantly developed greater strength.

Progressive resistance is the basic idea behind weight training. As you work with weights, you get stronger and can easily do the repetitions called for in each exercise. When those movements get easy, it's necessary to increase the weight you use and make the movements harder again. If you don't continue to add resistance, you won't continue to gain strength.

MUSCLE GROUPS

The body consists of five major muscle groups. Many exercises and their variations isolate specific muscles. Other movements work an entire muscle group or several muscles at the same time. Some exercises benefit the whole body.

The muscle groups are:
1. Torso—neck, upper back, shoulders, chest
2. Hips, lower back, and buttocks
3. Arms—biceps, triceps, forearms, wrists
4. Abdominals, upper and lower
5. Legs—thighs, hamstrings, calves, ankles

REPETITIONS

Each exercise is done a certain number of times or repetitions, usually 6 to 10.

SETS

Sets are groups of repetitions. Most exercises are done in 2 or 3 sets of 6 to 10 repetitions.

CIRCUIT

It's best to go through one complete series of exercises doing one set of each and then go back and do the complete sequence again. This is called circuit training and it allows the muscles to recover.

SPEED

Slow and steady is the best way to perform most weight-training exercises. There is some research to show that the speed of your movements is immaterial; but it's still not a good idea to throw the weight up and down as fast as you can, because you can strain muscles needlessly with irregular jerks and tugs.

8
Part I—Pre- (Post-) Run Warmups with Weights — 7 Minutes

Runners are experts at warming up. Well, if not experts, then at least knowledgeable; that is, they know that warming up before exercise is a good thing. They may even know the "why" of warming up. It's the "how" that seems to elude them. I'm not making fun of warming up before running, because it's important; but it often seems that the point of most warmup gyrations is to be really creative, if not bizarre, with running itself being only secondary.

You may have heard the sports expression, "They left their game in the locker room." I have the feeling that some runners leave their race somewhere behind the starting line in the warmup area. I've seen people running all-out sprints before the start of a marathon when energy conservation is critical. They are usually the same people who sprint out at the gun and the same people you pass after 3 or 4 miles, belly-up by the side of the road.

The "why" of warmup before exercise is simple. Cold, stiff muscles are subject to strains, pulls, and tears when called on to contract quickly while cold. Slowly stretching them, getting the blood flowing to the muscle tissue, pushing the blood through the veins to the heart, are good and positive things to do. But in distance running it's hardly necessary to do a "Nureyev" before hitting the streets or the track. The body and the muscles will warm naturally if you start running slowly, and in 3 minutes or less the cardiovascular system will be using all the oxygen it can get.

Physiologists have known for years that more than 15 minutes spent warming the muscles is wasted. Five to 7 minutes is usually enough. On the other hand, if you warm up and wait more than 15 minutes to start exercising, you'll have to start warming up all over again.

Warming up for weight training is a little different. Most of the movements performed in a typical workout require quick bursts of energy and are done without oxygen; that is, they're anaerobic. But as you continue to do the anaerobic movements with little rest they can reach the aerobic level.

Warmup is supposed to be sensible, slow and progressive. It basically serves one purpose—to raise the temperature of the muscles so that they will be loose and prepared for whatever work is to come. The warmup is not an end in itself.

This routine can be used before running as a 7-minute warmer or after running as a cool down. This whole sequence will completely warm and stimulate your body for running or the weight exercises that follow. The stretches and twists will work the sides, lower back, shoulders, and neck. The toe touches work the lower back and begin to stretch the hamstrings. Thrusts are particularly good for the frontal thighs, ankles, and knees. Sit-ups and leg raises are for the stomach, back, and hips.

Note: These exercises are based on the assumption that you are already in good physical condition. If that's not the case, begin by doing only half of the suggested repetitions.

THE RIGHT WEIGHT

Unfortunately there is no scientific way to choose the right weight to use for each exercise. Individual variations in strength and body type are just too great to say that if you are 5 feet 7 inches tall and weigh 160 pounds you should be able to handle 50 pounds for this or that exercise.

The choice will require some experimentation and may take a few minutes. You should try different poundages on the bar or the dumbbells until you can just do the suggested number of repetitions. If you can do them too easily, you need more weight; if they are too hard, take some weight off. At first, until you get used to handling the weights, it's probably better to go for a little lighter weight. You'll soon be able to determine poundages quite easily.

OVERHEAD-SIDE STRETCHES WITH DUMBBELL

Take a light dumbbell (just the dumbbell bar, if that's all you can handle at first) and hold it at arms length directly over your head. Keep your back straight, your head up, and your feet about shoulder width apart. Check to make sure your elbows are straight. Now bend to the right side trying to form an angle at the waist and not a "C." Go over as far as you can, feeling the stretch in the left side. Return to the starting position and repeat the movement to the other side. Bend 20 times to each side.

Time: 1 minute
Figures 2 and 3

TWISTS WITH DUMBBELL

Using the same weight as you did for the first exercise, take the same starting position. This time twist the upper body as far as you can to the right. You'll feel the and repeat twisting to the left. Move your hips as little as possible and keep your elbows close to your ears. Twist 20 times to each side.

Time: 1 minute
Figure 4

TOE TOUCHES WITH BAR OR DUMBBELL

Hold at least a 5-pound dumbbell or the bar at arms length in front of you. Your feet should be about 6 inches apart. Bend over slowly from the waist allowing the

Figure 2 / Figure 3: Overhead-side stretches with dumbbell

Figure 4: Twists with dumbbell (see p. 42)

weight to pull you down until you can touch the floor. Keep your legs as straight as possible and try to end up with your back parallel to the floor. If you can't make it all the way down, don't worry. Your muscles will eventually stretch until you can. After touching the floor, slowly uncurl and come back to a standing position and square your shoulders. Do 20 repetitions.

Time: 1 minute
Figures 5 and 6

THRUSTS WITH BAR

Stand straight with the bar resting on the base of your neck and shoulders. Your feet should be about 6 inches apart. Beginning with your right leg, stride forward about 2 feet, planting your foot firmly. Let your left heel come off the floor and touch the floor with your left knee if you can (touch but don't bang it). Push back up to a standing position and repeat with the left leg striding out. If you can't touch the floor with your knee, you may have to step out a little farther. Do this exercise slowly at first, because it's easy to lose your balance. You'll feel the stretch in the quadriceps on the front of the thigh, but this exercise also warms the hip joints, knees, and ankles. Do 10 thrusts for each leg.

Time: 2 minutes
Figures 7 and 8

SIT-UPS WITH WEIGHT

These bent-knee sit-ups can be done with a slant board (as shown) or by tucking your toes under anything solid—a chair, bed, dresser, whatever. Place either a light barbell plate or a light dumbbell behind your neck and curl up slowly, using the stomach muscles only (if you feel it in your thighs, you aren't using your stomach

Figure 5: Toe touches with bar or dumbbell (see p. 42)

Figure 6

Figure 7/ Figure 8: Thrusts with bar (see p. 45)

Figure 9: Sit-ups with weight (see p. 45)

Figure 10

Figure 11: Leg raises (see p. 54)

Figure 12

muscles) until you can touch your elbows to your knees. Lower yourself slowly back to the board or the floor. Do 10 repetitions, rest a few seconds, and do 10 more.

This same exercise can also be done by curling up only halfway, holding for a count of 2, and lowering yourself back to the starting position.

Time: 1 minute
Figures 9 and 10

LEG RAISES

Leg raises are also for the stomach, and they can be done in addition to, or instead of, sit-ups. Lie on the board or flat on the floor with your arms extended behind your head. You can hold a barbell or something solid if you need to. Keep your legs together and your knees straight. Slowly raise your legs as high as you can toward the vertical. Lower them slowly until your heels are almost touching the floor. Repeat 10 times, rest 10 seconds, and do another 10. Leave your shoes on for added weight.

Time: 1 minute.
Figures 11 and 12

9
Part II—
Lifting on a Running Day—
10 Minutes

T he five exercises in this section are basically whole-body exercises. They work all of the major muscle groups and most of the minor muscles as well. If you did only these five regularly you would develop significant new strength and stamina. Add these to the next two sections, however, and you have a complete workout that exercises the entire body, then places added emphasis on the legs and then the upper body.

SQUATS

Squats, or deep knee bends, may be the best single exercise anyone can do. They work the front and back of the thighs, the buttocks, and the lower back; and they cause an immediate increase in the pulse rate.

Stand close to the bar with your feet about shoulder width apart. Squat down and grasp the bar with an overhand grip (palms down), hands at shoulder width, and shoulders a little ahead of the bar. Slowly raise the bar in a line parallel with your body until you can tuck your elbows under it and raise it to chest level. Press it straight up from that point and then lower it softly behind your head until it rests comfortably on your shoulders and neck. Make sure you're well balanced. Spread your feet wider if necessary and move your hands out on the bar if you need to. Next, squat slowly, and keep your back as straight as you can and your head up. Stop when your thighs are roughly parallel with the floor. Raise back up to the standing position. It won't hurt to practice a little on this one, because balance is very important.

When you've completed your squats, take the bar off your shoulders the same way you put it on—press it over your head, lower it to your chest, and then to the floor bending your knees as you do.

Sets: 2
Reps: 8 to 10
Time: 2 minutes
Figures 13 and 14

OVERHEAD PRESSES

The press, sometimes called the military press, is another good whole-body exercise, but it is most beneficial for the triceps and the deltoids (the delta-shaped muscles at the point where the arm meets the shoulder). Raise the barbell to chest level the same way you did getting ready for the squats. When you are steady and well balanced, press the bar straight up over your head until your arms are fully extended. Lower it back to the chest. Make sure your back is as straight as you can get it, and keep your head up.

Sets: 2
Reps: 6.
Time: 2 minutes
Figures 15 and 16

POWER CLEANS

The power clean is the same as an overhead press, only the entire movement of picking the bar up from the floor to the arms-extended position is done together. Pull the weight off the floor, along a plane parallel with the body, tucking the elbows under and then smoothly pressing the bar from the shoulders to the overhead position. Lower it back to the floor for each rep. You'll feel this one in your legs, arms, stomach, shoulders, buttocks, neck, and back. The only thing keeping the power clean from being the perfect exercise is that it doesn't get the pulse up as fast as the squat.

Sets: 2
Reps: 6
Time: 2 minutes
Figures 17, 18, and 19

GOOD MORNINGS

The origin of this name is obscure because it's a rather difficult exercise that puts a strain on the frontal thighs, the buttocks, the hamstrings, the stomach, and the lower back. Place the bar on your shoulders as you've done for previous exercises and spread your feet a bit more than shoulder width apart. Keep the back straight and the head up while bending forward at the waist. Go down until your back is parallel with the floor, hold for a count of two and then slowly raise back to the starting point. It may take you awhile to get the bar in a comfortable position and balanced, so practice a couple of times to get just the right feel.

Sets: 2
Reps: 6
Time: 2 minutes
Figures 20 and 21

Figure 13/ Figure 14: Squats (see p. 55)

Figure 15: **Overhead presses** (see p. 56)

Figure 16

Figure 17/ Figure 18/ Figure 19: Power cleans (see p. 57)

Figure 20: Good mornings (see p. 57)

Figure 21

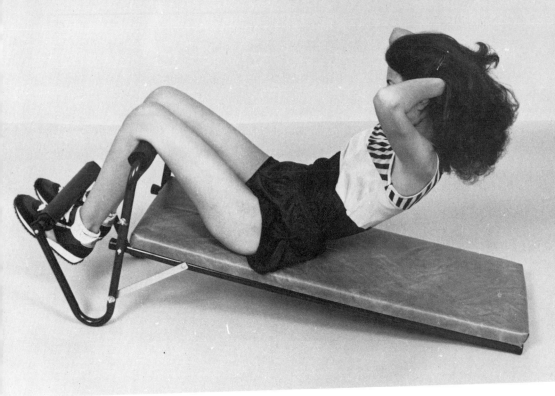

Figure 22: Crunch sit-ups

CRUNCH SIT-UPS

Crunches are done in the same way as regular bent-leg sit-ups; but instead of going all the way up to touch your knees, just go halfway up very slowly and lower yourself back very slowly. This is particularly good for the lower abdominal area. For additional intensity, put a small dumbbell behind your neck.

Sets: 2
Reps: 10
Time: 3 minutes
Figure 22

This basic sequence should take no more than 12 minutes. You will see as you move through it at a steady pace that your pulse rate will continue to rise. This will put you in a perfect range to go out for a short run if you feel like it. The warmups (7 minutes), this sequence (12 minutes), and a 10- to 15-minute run make a very complete workout. If you do all three you will have done the equivalent of about a 6-mile run.

10
Part III —
A Workout for Off-Days —
20 Minutes

Begin this sequence with the warmups followed by the five exercises in Part II. Don't try to do it all just before or just after running. This routine of ten exercises is designed for those off-days or for a period of 6 to 8 hours either before or after a rather short run.

DUMBBELL SWING

Take dumbbell in both hands and raise it to arms length above your head, keeping your back straight. Spread your legs far enough apart to allow the dumbbell to swing through. Slowly swing the dumbbell from the overhead position in a wide arc bending forward as the weight reaches chest level and then continue to bend while swinging the weight between your legs as far as you can with comfort. Follow the same arc and bring the weight back up to the overhead position. This exercises the whole body but especially the back and the buttocks.

Sets: 2
Reps: 20
Time: 4 minutes
Figures 23 and 24

Figure 23/Figure 24: Dumbbell swing (see p. 67)

Figure 25 / Figure 26: Alternate dumbbell press

ALTERNATE DUMBBELL PRESS

Take dumbbells in both hands and bring them to the shoulders, palms in. Back straight and head up, press the dumbbell in your right hand until your arm is fully extended. Keep the other dumbbell on your shoulder. As you begin to lower the right arm, begin to press the left until it's overhead. Continue to alternate. This exercise works the shoulders and the triceps.

Sets: 3
Reps: 10 with each arm
Time: 5 minutes
Figures 25 and 26

SQUAT JUMP

Prepare for this exercise by putting the bar on your shoulders as you did for the squat. Begin with the back straight, head up, and feet fairly close together. Jump off the floor a few inches and at the same time move your right foot forward and your left foot back, landing on the balls of your feet. Don't jump so high that you lose your balance or land awkwardly. As soon as you touch down, jump up again and reverse your legs so that the left foot is forward and the right foot is back. This is a strenuous exercise and should not ever be done with much weight; but it is great for the thighs and calves and it gets the heart pumping. Use the bar only as long as you feel comfortable.

Sets: 2
Reps: 8
Time: 2 minutes
Figures 27, 28, and 29

Figure 27: Squat jump (see p. 70)

UPRIGHT ROWS

Bend your knees and pick up the bar with palms down and hands about 4 inches apart. Stand up and raise the bar to arms-extended position. The rows are done by bringing the bar straight up on a plane parallel with the body until it's right under your chin. The elbows will be pointing out at almost right angles to the body and a little more than shoulder high. Keep the back straight and the head up. This is especially good for the shoulders and neck.

Sets: 3
Reps: 10
Time: 4 minutes
Figures 30 and 31

TOE RAISES

You can either put the bar on your shoulders for this one, hold it at arms length in front of you, or use dumbbells at your sides. Stand straight, head up, with your feet a few inches apart. Raise up as high as you can on your toes and then lower your heels to the floor. This is a calf exercise.

Sets: 3
Reps: 10
Time: 4 minutes
Figure 32

The warm-ups and ten exercises you have now done will provide a total workout that will stimulate muscular growth and increase the pulse rate to a level that will give you the same training effect as a sustained, vigorous run.

Figure 28: Squat jump (see p. 70)

Figure 29

Figure 30: Upright rows (see p. 72)

Figure 31

Figure 32: Toe raises (see p. 72)

11
Part IV—
Lifting Instead of
Running—
25 Minutes

T ry to remember what people did for exercise ten years ago. Men played golf, tennis, bowled, tossed an occasional softball, went swimming, and watched sports on television. Women did just about the same things.

Then running came on the scene in the mid-seventies and people hit the streets—especially men, because they heard that running was good for the heart. If there is anything that the American male fears more than his boss, it's a heart attack.

A lot of people even got to like running as well, because it took off weight and made them feel better mentally and emotionally. If it wasn't fun, at least it seemed virtuous and rewarding.

Today, a lot of people actually run for fun because running has become part of their life style. But more people, still mostly men, are on the move because they are running (no pun intended) from heart attacks, or at least they think they are. After all, even the American Heart Association, a group that rarely sprints into controversy, has taken the position that it "is at least prudent to exercise." And further, they say that though "exercise training does not seem to stop hardening of the arteries, it does appear to render the atherosclerotic process less apt to lead to a heart attack."

It may not be fair to say that everyone runs in fear, but the Perrier research found that "75 percent of the exercising public felt that the most imoprtant type of exercise for physical fitness is that which strengthens the heart and improves blood circulation."

Which brings us to the newly discovered and now venerated "training effect." All serious runners know about the training effect, and for some reason they think the only way to get a case of it is to run.

The training effect was not a brainchild of some sports medics who came on the scene in the 1970s but a resurrection of some research done in the early 1930s by a group of Scandinavian physiologists, who discovered that vigorous activity improved cardiovascular fitness. They showed that regular, heavy exercise brought about adjustments in the body's circulatory and respiratory systems and lowered the heart rate. Having found this, they increased the exercise load and learned that the system continued to adapt and, more importantly, that when the exercise was again performed at the original level the heart rate of the exerciser was lowered, meaning he could handle work with less effort. This is now called the training effect.

But how do you get a dose of training effect? Simply raise your heart rate to 60 to 80 percent of its maximum (about 130 to 140 beats a minute for most adults) and keep it there for 10 to 12 minutes, three times a week. This type of stress can increase the strength of the heart.

This means that running, swimming, biking, skiing, and jumping rope can improve the heart's fitness if they are performed with, as the *Physical Fitness Research Digest* says, "sufficiently severe and prolonged effort to require a definite adjustment of circulation and respiration to the effort."

"Severe" and "prolonged" are the key words, because if the heart rate doesn't go up, there is no training effect. And, of course, it has to happen at least three times a week. It becomes obvious then that bowling, golf, even tennis and racquetball, don't benefit the heart because they just aren't intense enough. And jogging slowly is probably not intense enough either.

This intensity factor is the reason most medical people still say that weight training is a good conditioner for the muscles but that it isn't aerobic enough to create a training effect. They are right if the weight lifting is done at a leisurely pace with plenty of rest between sets.

But there is also strong medical evidence indicating that weight training, performed at an *intense* level, is also a cardiovascular conditioner. One of the world's foremost authorities on work and exercise physiology, Dr. Per-Olof Astrand, says, "Practical experience has shown that work with large muscle groups for three to five minutes followed by rest or light physical activity for an equal length of time, then further work, is an effective method of training the heart." He goes on to say that the training doesn't have to be maximal during the workouts and that you don't have to be exhausted when you finish to have achieved the desired effect.

Some further proof was produced in the late seventies by Dr. James Peterson in an experiment with highly trained athletes at West Point. Peterson found that 6 weeks of weight-training exercises that limited the rest between exercises to a few seconds created the kind of intensity that "significantly improved the cardiovascular condition of the subjects." He says the program proved that "contrary to widespread opinion not only will a properly conducted program of strength training produce increases in muscular strength but will also significantly improve an individual's level of cardiovascular conditioning."

But what does all this really prove for the dedicated runner who plans to keep running for the heart, through sleet and storm and howling gale, even the dark of night? Only this: Weight training with intensity can substitute for running as a heart conditioner.

No one is saying don't run. Heaven forbid. The point is that running doesn't have to be an obsession and that foregoing the day's outing in favor of the weights won't throw the old ticker into arrhythmic drum rolls. So relax and try the routines described in this section instead of running. Try a couple of times, even more. If you give it a chance, you'll find that you will get the same heart benefits but you'll get much more as well. After a few intense workouts you'll find that you have become a greatly improved runner. Your step will be firmer, your forward thrust will be stronger and more enduring, and your heart will be light.

The exercises in this section, combined with those in the warm-up section and Parts II and III, make an ideal 25- to 40-minute workout that will put all the body's large muscles into play and make it easy to reach a heart rate of at least 130 beats a minute and hold it there for 10 to 12 minutes.

There is no playing around here. The idea is to move from set to set and exercise to exercise with little or no rest. You won't be using the same set of muscles twice in a row, so all the muscles will have the necessary time to recover their strength. If you find yourself needing rest between sets, just do some light calisthenics—toe touching, side bends, side-straddle hops, even sit-ups. Keep moving and you'll soon work up a sweat that's equal to any half-hour run you ever took, and you'll find your breath a little hard to come by. Of course, that's what it's all about.

Note: If you decide to do all 20 of the exercises in this book at one time, don't, repeat, do not, plan to run on the same day. In fact, the complete workout in this section alone will be a more than adequate substitute for your run. The amount of energy expended is high, the cardiovascular effect is there, and you will have successfully stressed your whole body.

BENT-OVER ROWS

Bend over and pick up the bar with a grip that is slightly more than shoulder width. Keep your back parallel to the floor, your head up, and legs straight. Bring the bar directly up to your chest with elbows flaring out. This is good for the shoulders and back.

Sets: 3
Reps: 8
Time: 4 minutes
Figures 33 and 34

CURLS

This exercise is mostly for the biceps, but it's also good for the back. Bend over and pick up the bar with an underhanded grip (palms up) and stand up with it at arms length against your thighs. Now, slowly curl the bar up to the chest keeping the back straight. Lower the weight back down until the arms are fully extended again. You'll find that after several curls you'll have a tendency to throw the hips forward and arch the back in order to get the weight moving. Try to keep the "cheating" to a minimum and make the arms do the bulk of the work. Note: This exercise can be performed with either a bar or dumbbells.

Sets: 3
Reps: 8
Time: 4 minutes
Figures 35 and 36

Figure 33: Bent-over rows

Figure 34

Figure 35: Curls (see p. 82)

Figure 36

TRICEPS EXTENSIONS

You can do this exercise on a bench if you have one, or on the floor, or standing. With hands about 8 inches apart, bring the weight to the chest and then press it overhead, with arms fully extended and elbows near your ears. Using the elbows as a lever, lower the weight as far as you can behind your head. Bring it back up to the overhead position. Keep the back straight, head up, and upper arms motionless.

Sets: 3
Reps: 6
Time: 4 minutes
Figures 37 and 38

LATERAL RAISES

Hold a dumbbell in each hand at your sides, palms facing in. Raise the weights directly away from the sides until they are about shoulder high. The back is straight, and the head up. This is good for the shoulders and back.

Sets: 3
Reps: 8
Time: 5 minutes
Figures 39 and 40

Figure 37: Triceps extensions   **Figure 38**

Figure 39: Lateral raises (see p. 86)

Figure 40

Figure 41: Bench press (see p. 92)

Figure 42

BENCH PRESS

Lying on your bench or the floor, begin with the weight at arms length directly over the chest, hands about shoulder width in an overhand grip. Lower the bar to your chest keeping the elbows out to the sides. Then press it up to arms length again. If you use the floor for this exercise, try not to push up with your elbows. This is an arm and chest exercise and probably the best of all exercises for the chest.

Sets: 3
Reps: 10
Time: 5 minutes
Figures 41 and 42

12
Motivation

There are days when you have to force yourself out the door to run. One reason for this occasional lapse in motivation is the lack of progress sensed in day-to-day running. You just can't see progress and you often can't feel it either.

Training with weights is a different matter. You won't see progress after every workout, but you will be able to see it in the mirror every 2 or 3 weeks. That flabbiness in the triceps will begin to disappear, the stomach will get harder and leaner, and there will be new muscle development in the thighs. When you run you'll be less tense in the shoulders and neck, and any tendency to cramp will disappear.

You'll be running more easily, even breathing more easily. You'll actually be making quantum leaps in running, and at the same time you'll be developing muscle that you can actually see.

This is the one area where weight lifting is more gratifying than running—and it's a motivational factor that will keep you going back for more.